The Modern Book of Muslim Names

The Modern Book of
Muslim Names

Hansib Publications

Published by Hansib Publications, 2001

Hansib Publications Limited
P.O. Box 34621
London E17 4GL

Orchard Road
Royston
Hertfordshire SG8 5HA

ISBN 1 870518 73 X

Production by Books of Colour, Hertfordshire

Cover by Graphic Resolutions, Hertfordshire

Printed by Interprint Limited, Malta

PUBLISHER'S NOTE

*Every effort has been made to authenticate both the meaning and the
transliteration of the names included in this book. However, if you
are aware of spellings or translations which differ from the ones
published or, indeed, if you know of a name which has not been
included, we shall be pleased to hear from you. This will prove
invaluable when compiling any future editions.*

The Modern Book of Muslim Names

Boys

Abbas
The fury of a lion

Abbood see Abbud

Abbud
Worshipper

Abd see Abdul

Abdul
Servant, devotee

Abdullah
*Servant of Allah, one of
the attributes of the
Prophet Muhammad*

Abeed see Abid

Abid
Devotee

Aboo see Abu

Abrar
Pious people, saints

Abu
Father

Adal
Fair, just

Adam
*Wheat-coloured, the
name of the first man*

**Adeeb
see Adib**

Adeel see Adil

Adib
Writer, scholar

Adil
*Even-handed, just, one of
the attributes of the
Prophet Muhammad*

Adnan
In paradise

Afan
Humble

Afdhal
Most excellent

Afeef see Afif

Afif
Chaste

**Afouw
see Afuw**

Afqar
Modest

Afsar
Good

Aftab
The sun

Afuw
Forgiving

Afzal
Kindness

Agha
Chief, master

Ahad
Unique

Ahmad
Worthy of praise, one of the attributes of the Prophet Muhammad

Ahmed see Ahmad

Ahsan
Virtuous

Aibaq
Messenger

Aimal
Handsome

Aiman see Ayman

Aiysh
Prosperous

Ajmal
Most handsome

Ajwad
Most generous

Akbar
Honourable, most pious

Akeed see Akid

Akeef see Akif

Akher
Another

Akhgar
Spark

Akhlaq
Pure of heart

Akhtar
Stars

Akid
Certain, sure

Akif
To worship Allah in solitude

Akmal
Perfect

Akram
Gracious, kind

Alal
Comforter

Alam
The world, the universe

Alavi
Divine

Aleem see Alim

Ali
*The highest, sublime,
honourable*

Alim
Learned, wise

Aliy see Ali

Altaf
Gift, favour

**Altoon
see Altun**

Altun
Gold

Alvi see Alavi

Aman
Protection, safety

Amanat
Safe-keeping

Amar
To live for a long time

Ameel see Amil

Ameen see Amin

Ameer see Amir

Amil
Hopeful

Amin
*Faithful, trustworthy,
one of the attributes of
the Prophet Muhammad*

Amir
*Prince, ruler, one of the
attributes of the Prophet
Muhammad*

Amiyn see Amin

Amjad
*Noble, one with
grandeur*

Amar
Command, request

Anas
Man, friend, affection

Aneeq see Aniq

Anees see Anis

Aniq
Elegant

Anis
Close friend

**Anjoom
see Anjum**

Anjum
Stars

Ansar
To help in battle

Anwar
*Most brilliant, the
brightest light*

Aqa
Master

Aqah see Aqa

**Aqeeb
see Aqib**

**Aqeel
see Aqil**

Aqib
*Final, one of the
attributes of the Prophet
Muhammad*

Aqil
Sensible, wise

Aqmar
Moon

Arafat
*Unity, place of
pilgrimage*

**Areeb
see Arib**

**Areef
see Arif**

Areej see Arij

Arib
Wise, intelligent

Arif
*Expert, one who
possesses knowledge of
Allah and His kingdom*

Arij
Fragrant, sweet-smelling

Armaghan
Gift

Arman
Hope, aspiration

Arsalan see Arslan

Arshad
The most upright and honest

Arshaq
Handsome or, literally, one with a befitting height and a well proportioned body

Arslan
Lion

Arwah
Spirits, souls

Asad
Lion

Asaf
Sorrow

Asdaq
Truthful

Aseef see Asif

Aseel see Asil

Aseem see Asim

Asgar see Asghar

Asghar
Younger, smallest

Asheeq see Ashiq

Ashfaq
Kindness, blessings

Ashiq
Suitor

Ashraf
Most noble, cultured

Asif
Intelligent

Asil
Pure, original, genuine

Asim
Protector, guardian

Aslam
Safe, one who is protected from calamities and misfortunes

Asmar
Brown

Asuman
The sky

Aswad
Black

Ata
Gift, generosity

Atahiya
Salute

Ataib
Pure

Ateef see Atif

Ateek see Atiq

Ateeq see Atiq

Ateer see Atir

Athar
Meticulously neat and clean, most pious

Atheer see Athir

Ather see Athar

Athir
Air

Atif
Compassionate, affectionate

Atik see Atiq

Atiq
Liberated

Atir
Aromatic

Attar
Perfumer

Atyab
Refined, excellent

Auj
Zenith

Aun
Assistance, guidance

Aurangzeeb see Aurangzib

Aurangzib
Ornament of the throne, the name of the most magnificent of the Mughal emperors

Aus
Wolf

Awab
Guided to the path of righteousness, one of the attributes of the Prophet Muhammad

Awad
Reward

Awal
First

Awan
Helper

Awn see Aun

Awrangzeb see Aurangzib

Awrangzeeb see Aurangzib

Ayman
Lucky

Ayoob see Ayub

Ayub
Patient, enduring

Ayyub see Ayub

Azad
Independent

Azam
Great, exalted

Azeem see Azim

Azeez see Aziz

Azfar
Winner, victor

Azhar
The most apparent, the most illuminated

Azim
Mighty, dignified

Aziz
Respected, beloved, powerful

Azmat
Grandeur

Azzam
Determined

B

Baber see Babur

**Baboor
see Babur**

Babur
*Tiger, the name of the
first great Mughal
emperor*

Badee see Badi

Badi
Novel, wonderful

Badr
The full moon

Baha
Magnificence, elegance

Baheer see Bahir

Bahee see Bahi

Bahi
Splendid

Bahir
Dazzling, brilliant

Bahiy see Bahi

Bahr
The sea

Baith
To resurrect

Baiyth see Baith

Bakht
Luck

Bakoor see Bakur

Bakr
First born

Bakur
Maturity, wisdom

**Baleegh see
Baligh**

Baligh
Eloquent, learned

Baqee see Baqi

Baqi
Eternal

Baqeer see Baqir

Baqir
Fierce lion, learned

Barakat
Blessings

Baree see Bari

Bari
Creator, deity

Barkat
Prosperity, blessing

Barq
Lightning

Barraq
Bright, shining

Baseel see Basil

**Baseem
see Basim**

Baseer see Basir

Baseet see Basit

**Baseerat
see Basirat**

Bashar see Bashir

**Basharat
see Basharat**

Basharat
Good news, glad tidings

**Basheer
see Bashir**

Bashir
*The bringer of glad
tidings, one of the
attributes of the Prophet
Muhammad*

**Bashshar
see Bashir**

Basil
Brave, strong

Basim
Smiling, happy

Basir
Wise, shrewd

Basirat
Perception

Basit
*One who bestows
prosperity*

**Bassam
see Basim**

Batal
Brave, champion

**Bateen
see Batin**

Batin
Hidden

Behlol
Jovial

Bilal
Water, freshness

Birr
Generous, righteous

Bisher
Evidence

Bishr see Bisher

Burhan
Proof, evidence

D

Daa
One who welcomes, one of the attributes of the Prophet Muhammad

Daim
Ever lasting, eternal

Dag
Mountain

Daiyan
Judge, protector

Dalair
Brave, strong

Daleel see Dalil

Dalil
Teacher, guide

**Dameer
see Damir**

Damir
Conscience

Dana
Wise, intelligent

Daneesh
see Danish

Danish
Knowledgeable

Darya
The ocean

Dastgir
Helper

Daulah
see Dawlah

Dawlah
Riches, happiness

Deel see Dil

Deen
Faith, religion

Demeer see Demir

Demir
Iron

Dhahabee
see Dhahabi

Dhahabi
Golden, precious

Dhaigham
see Dirgham

Dhakee
see Dhaki

Dhaki
Clever

Dhakeer
see Dhakir

Dhakir
One who acknowledges Allah

Dhameen
see Dhamin

Dhamin
Guarantor, helper

Dhiya
Brilliance, splendour

Dil
Heart

Dilawar
Brave, strong

Dilshad
Happiness

Din
see Deen

Dirgham
Lion

Diya
Splendour

Door see Dur

Dost
Friend

Dur
Pearl, gem

Ehsan
A gift to the poor, blessing

Ehtamad
Trust

Eijaz see Ijaz

Eizaz
Respectability

Fadee see Fadi

Fadeel see Fadil

Fadhal see Fazal

**Fadheel
see Fadil**

Fadhil see Fadil

Fadhl
Wisdom, virtue

Fadi
Redeemer, saviour

Fadil
Accomplished

Fadl see Fadhl

Fahd
Cheetah

**Faheem
see Fahim**

Fahim
Intelligent, learned

Faidh
Generosity, favour

Faiq
Overwhelming, excellent

Faisal
*Arbitrator, impartial
judge*

Faiz
Reward, victorious

**Fakheer
see Fakhir**

Fakhir
Luxurious, precious

Fakhr
*Glory, someone to be
proud of*

**Fakhree
see Fakhri**

Fakhri
Proud, glorious

Fala see Falah

Falah
Success

**Faleeb
see Falib**

Falib
Victor

Faqeeh
see Faqih

Faqeer see Faqir

Faqih
Knowledgeable,
understanding

Faqir
One who leads a pious
life

Farah
Happy, content

Faraj
Peace of mind

Farasat
Discerning

Faraz
Zenith

Fareed see Farid

Farees see Faris

Fareh see Farah

Farhan
Joyful

Farhat
Happiness, joy

Farid
Unique, a pearl

Farih see Farhan

Faris
Knight, soldier,
horseman

Farooq see Faruq

Faruq
One who distinguishes
between right and wrong

Fasahat
Fluency, smoothness

Faseeh
see Faseh

Faseh
Abundance

Fasih
Educated

Fattah see Fatih

Fateen see Fatin

Fath
Victory

Fathee see Fathi

Fathi
Freedom, liberation

Fatih
Conqueror

Fatin
Aware, clever

Fattah see Fatin

Fattan
Lovable, charming, bright

Fauz see Fawz

**Fauzee
see Fawzi**

**Fauzi
see Fawzi**

Fawwaz
Successful

Fawz
Triumph

**Fawzee
see Fawzi**

Fawzi
Victorious

Fayad
Most generous and bountiful

Fayd
Favour

Fayeeq see Faiq

Fayiq see Faiq

**Faysal
see Faisal**

**Fayyadh
see Fayad**

Fayz see Faiz

Fazal
Good fortune, luck

Feeda see Fida

**Ferhan
see Farhan**

Feroz
Turquoise

Fiaz see Fayad

Fida
Sacrifice

Fidha see Fida

Firas
Perception, insight

Firasah
To perceive, to have insight

Firdoos see Firdous

Firdous
A garden in Heaven

Foowad see Fuad

Fowad see Fuad

Fowwaz
Winner

Fuad
The heart

Fudhail see Fadhl

Furqan
To distinguish truth from falsehood

Furrukh
Young birds

Furukh see Furrukh

Futuh
Victories

Fuwad see Fuad

Fuyoodh see Fuyudh

Fuyudh
Favours

Ghaffar
Most forgiving, most merciful

Ghaffur
see Ghaffar

Ghafoor
see Ghaffar

Ghafur
see Ghaffar

Ghalib
Conqueror

Ghanee
see Ghani

Ghaneem
see Ghanim

Ghani
Prosperous, self-sufficient

Ghanim
To gain, successful

Ghaus see Ghauth

Ghauth
Helper or, literally, redresser of grievances

Ghawth
see Ghauth

Ghazee
see Ghazi

Ghazi
Soldier, warrior

Ghiyath
Deliverance from hardship

Ghiyyas
see Ghiyath

Gholam
see Ghulam

Ghous
see Ghauth

Ghufran
Forgive, pardon

Ghulam
Servant

Golab see Gulab

Gul
Flower, flower bud

Gulab
A rose

Gulshan
Garden

Gulzar see Gulshan

Habeeb see Habib

Habeel see Habil

Habib
Beloved friend, one of the attributes of the Prophet Muhammad

Habil
Accomplished, able

Had
Chief, leader, one of the attributes of the Prophet Muhammad

Hadayat
Guidance, instruction

Hadee see Hadi

Hadhir see Hazir

Hadi
Leader, guide, one of the attributes of the Prophet Muhammad

Hafeez see Hafiz

Hafiz
Guardian, protector

Hafs
Lion cub

Haidar
Fierce lion

Hak see Haq

Hakam
Arbitrator, judge

**Hakeem
see Hakim**

Hakim
Philosopher, a wise man

Haleef see Halif

Haleem see Halim

Halif
Ally

Halim
*A patient man, one who
perseveres*

Hamaiz see Hamiz

Hamal
*A lamb, a very gentle
person*

Hamas
Enthusiasm

**Hamayat
see Himayat**

**Hamd
see Hamid**

**Hamdan
see Hamud**

**Hamdee
see Hamdi**

**Hamdha
see Hamzah**

Hamdi
Praiseworthy

**Hameed
see Hamid**

**Hameem
see Hamim**

**Hameez
see Hamiz**

Hamid
*One who praises
and glorifies Allah,
one of the attributes
of the Prophet
Muhammad*

Hamim
Close friend

Hamiz
Jovial, light-hearted

Hammad
see Hamid

Hammam
*Naturally helpful,
thoughtful*

Hammud
see Hamud

Hamood
see Hamud

Hamud
*One who constantly
praises and glorifies
Allah, one who is worthy
of praise*

Hamza
see Hamzah

Hamzah
Lion

Hanee
see Hani

Haneef
see Hanif

Hani
*Peace of mind,
contentment*

Hanif
*To cast aside falsehood
and profess the truth*

Hannan
Merciful, forgiving

Haq
The truth

Haqani
Correct, proper, follower

Haqq see Haq

Haqqani
see Haqani

Haque see Haq

Harb
War

Hareef see Harif

Harif
Warm

Haris
Ploughman, farmer

Haroon see Harun

Haroun
see Harun

Harun
The wealth of the universe, protector

Hasan
Pious, wise, excellent

Haseeb
see Hasib

Haseef see Hasif

Haseen
Handsome

Hasheem
see Hashim

Hashim
Generous, to distribute

Hashmat
Grace, respectability

Hasib
Of noble background

Hasif
One with sound judgement, wise

Hasin
Decisive

Hasrat
Desire, ambition

Hassan see Hasan

Hateem see Hatim

Hatim
Judge

Hayat
Life

Haydar
see Haidar

Haydara
Lion

Hayee see Hayi

Hayi
Immortal, eternal

Haytham
Eagle

Hayyan
Energetic, full of life

Hazeem
see Hazim

Hazeeq see Haziq

Hazeer see Hazir

Hazeez see Haziz

Hazim
Discreet

Haziq
Expert, skilled

Hazir
Present, available

Haziz
Fortunate

Hazn
Sorrow

**Hesham
see Hisham**

Hidayat
Guidance, righteousness

Hifz
To memorise, to preserve

Hilal
Crescent moon

Hilmee see Hilmi

Hilmi
Wise

Himayat
Protection, defence

Hisham
Generosity

Hobab see Hubab

Hosam
Sword

Hubab
Friend, companion

Hulayl see Hilal

**Humaid
see Hamid**

Humam
Courageous, generous

Humayun
Blessed, revered

Hurairah
Kitten

**Hurayra
see Hurairah**

**Husain
see Hussain**

Husam
Sword

**Husayn
see Hussain**

Husn
Elegance

Husni see Hussain

Hussain
Pious, handsome

Hussayn
see Hussain

I

Ibraheem
see Ibrahim

Ibrahim
*Most affectionate father,
father of the people*

Idrees
see Idris

Idris
To read, teacher

Iffat
Pure

Iftakhar
see Iftikhar

Iftikhar
Honour, respectability

Ihsan
Kindness, sincerity

Ihtisham
Magnificence, glory

Ijaz
Miracle

Ikhlaq
Morals

Ikhlas
*Friendship, sincerity,
purity*

Ikram
Honouring, pay respects

Ikrima see Ikrimah

Ikrimah
Dove

Ilyas
Strong, brave

Imad
Support

Imam
Leader in prayer, guide

Iman
Faith, belief

Imdad
*Support, the spreading of
light during the day*

Imran
Cultured

Imtial
Difference

Imtiaz
Priviledge, wisdom

Imtiyaz see Imtiaz

Inam
To present a gift

Inayah
Care

Inayat
Favour

Insaf
Truth, justice

Iqbal
Good fortune

Iqtidar
Strength, power

Irfan
Acknowledgement

Irshad
*To guide to the right
path, to advocate what is
good*

Irtida
Satisfaction

Isam
Safeguard, protect

Ishaq
One who laughs

Ishfaq
Kind, forgiving,
compassionate

Ishrat
Together

Ishtiaq
Desire, fondness

Islam
The religon of
Muslims, to bow
one's head in
submission

Ismael
see Ismail

Ismail
One who obeys Allah

Ismat
Chastity

Israr
Secrets

Istifa
To choose, to prefer

Itimad
Faith, trust

Izam
Great people

Izaz
To respect and honour,
to raise to an exalted
position

Izhar
Declaration, opinion

Izz
Might, strength

J

Jabal
Mountain

Jabbar
Mighty, powerful, king

Jabir
To comfort, to console

Jabran
Reward, gift

Jafar
River

Jaffar see Jafar

Jah
Wealth

Jahangir
Conqueror of the world

Jahl
Ignorance

Jalal
Majesty, glory

Jaleel see Jalil

Jalib
Intention, desire

Jalil
Dignified, illustrious

Jalis
Companion, associate

Jamal
Good looking, good character

**Jameel
see Jamil**

Jami
Collector

Jamil
Handsome, attractive

**Jamooh
see Jamuh**

Jamshaid
Lights, illuminations

Jamuh
Brave, defiant

Jasir
Mighty

**Jauhar
see Jawhar**

Javaid
Lively, alive, eternal

**Javed
see Javaid**

**Javid
see Javaid**

Jawad
*Generous, charitable,
one of the attributes
of the Prophet
Muhammad*

Jawhar
*Gem, jewel,
essence*

Jawhari
Essential

**Jawwad
see Jawad**

Jibran
Reward

Jihad
Struggle, holy war

Jiyad
Excellent, pure

Jummal
Rope

Junaid
Warrior, army

Junayd see Junaid

Kabeer
see Kabir

Kabir
Great, immense, senior

Kafeel see Kafil

Kafil
Guarantor, responsible

Kaif
To enjoy

Kaleem
see Kalim

Kalil see Khalil

Kalim
Orator, speaker

Kamal
Perfection

Kamil
Perfect, complete

Karam
Kindness, generosity

Karamah
Dignity, nobility

Karamat
Excellence, magnificence

Kareem see Karim

Karim
Generous, merciful

Karrar
Peace

Kaseeb see Kasib

Kaseer see Kasir

Kashif
Explorer, discoverer

Kasib
Winner, to gain

Kasir
Powerful

Kathir
Ample, abundance

Kausar
*Fountain, a river in
Paradise*

Kauthar
see Kausar

Kazim
One who suppresses his anger, controlled

Kedar
Powerful

**Khabeer
see Khabir**

Khabir
Expert, knowledgeable, informer

**Khadhin
see Khazin**

Khadim
Aide, servant, helper

Khafid
To please

Khafiz
Humble

Khair
Charity, benevolence, good

Khairat
Help, assist

Khairee
Charitable

Khalaf
Heir, successor

Khaldun
Immortal

**Khaleel
see Khalil**

Khaleeq
The Creator, kind

Khalid
Eternal, permanent, one who remains strong

**Khalifa
see Khalifah**

Khalifah
Successor

Khalil
A sincere friend, one of the attributes of the Prophet Muhammad

Khalis
Original, clear, pure

Khan
Leader, chief

**Khateeb
see Khatib**

Khatib
Orator

Khatim
*Ring, one of the
attributes of Prophet
Muhammad*

Khatir
Heart, idea

Khayr see Khair

Khayri
Charitable

Khayyam
Tent-maker

Khayyir
Liberal, generous

Khazin
Treasurer

**Khidhar
see Khizar**

**Khidr
see Khizar**

Khizar
Guide, leader, evergreen

Khurram
Delight, happiness

**Khursheed
see Khurshid**

Khurshid
The sun

**Khushee
see Khushi**

Khushi
Joy, happiness

Khushnood
Happy, delighted

**Kibriya
see Kibriyah**

Kibriyah
*Dignity, glory,
splendour*

Kifayat
Self-sufficient

L

Labeeb see Labib

Labib
*To understand,
intelligent, clever*

Laeeq see Laiq

Lahab
Flame

Laiq
Deserving, worthy

Lateef see Latif

Latif
Gracious, kind

Layth
Lion

Layyin
Tender, resilient

Liaqah
Capable, merit

**Liaqat
see Liaqah**

**Liyaqah
see Liaqah**

Lootfi see Lutfi

Luqman
Wise, intelligent

Lutf
Kindness

Lutfi
Friendly, gentle

Madani
Civilised

Madeeh see Madih

Madih
*Praiseworthy,
commendable*

Madu
*Guest, one of the
attributes of Prophet
Muhammad*

Mahasin
Beautiful

**Mahboob
see Mahbub**

Mahbub
Beloved

**Mahdee
see Mahdi**

Mahdi
*Guided to the truth, one
of the attributes of the
Prophet Muhammad*

Mahdood
Limited

**Mahdoud
see Mahdood**

**Mahfooz
see Mahfuz**

Mahfuz
Protected, preserved

Mahir
Skilled, expert

**Mahmood
see Mahmud**

Mahmoon
Trustworthy

Mahmud
*Praiseworthy,
commendable, one
of the attributes
of the Prophet
Muhammad*

**Mahmun
see Mahmoon**

**Mahroof
see Mahruf**

Mahruf
Famous, notable

Mahzooz
see Mahzuz

Mahzuz
Lucky, fortunate

Maimoon
see Maymun

Majd
Glory

Majdi
Glorious, praiseworthy

Majeed see Majid

Majid
Honourable, illustrious

Makeen
see Makin

Makhdoom
Revered

Makin
Strong, firm

Mali
Noble, sublime

Malik see Maliq

Maliq
Master, lord

Maloom
see Malum

Malum
Known, one of the attributes of the Prophet Muhammad

Mamdooh
see Mamduh

Mamdouh
see Mamduh

Mamduh
Praised, glorified

Mamoon
see Mamun

Mamoun
see Mamun

Mamun
Trusted, dependable, one of the attributes of the Prophet Muhammad

Man
Benefit

Manazir
Competitor

Manfat
Gains, profit

Mannan
A great benefactor

Mansib
Grace, beauty

Mansoor
see Mansur

Mansur
Triumphant,
one of the attributes
of the Prophet
Muhammad

Manzar
Sight, view

Manzir
Guide

Manzoor
see Manzur

Manzur
Agreeable

Maqbool
see Maqbul

Maqbul
Accepted,
chosen

Maqsood
see Maqsud

Maqsud
Intention

Marghoob
see Marghub

Marghub
Desirable, pleasant

Marih
Lively, joyful

Marjan see Murjan

Maroof see Mahruf

Marwan
Kind

Marzooq
see Marzuq

Marzouq
see Marzuq

Marzuq
Fortunate, lucky

Maseeh
Blessed with piety

Mashhud
see Mashud

Mashkoor
see Mashkur

Mashkur
A person to whom one is indebted

Mashood
see Mashud

Mashooq
see Mashuq

Mashud
To attest, the day of judgement, one of the attributes of the Prophet Muhammad

Mashuq
Beloved

Masood
see Masud

Masoom
see Masum

Masoum
see Masum

Masroor
see Masrur

Masrour
see Masrur

Masrur
Pleased, happy, glad

Mastoor
see Mastur

Mastur
Protected

Masud
Lucky, happy

Masum
Innocent, protected

Mateen see Matin

Matin
Strong, of resolute mind, one of the attributes of the Prophet Muhammad

Matloob
see Matlub

Matlub
Desired, required

Maudood
see Mawdud

Maudoud
see Mawdud

Maula
Master

Mawdood
see Mawdud

Mawdud
Loving, desiring

Mawin
Deputy, helper, assistant

**Maymoon
see Maymun**

Maymun
Good fortune, blessed

Maysarah
Ease, comfort, restful

Mazhar
Spectacular

Mazin
Star

Meer see Mir

Miftah
Key

Minhaj
Path, road

Miqdam
Valiant, daring, brave

Mir
Chief, leader

Miraj
Ascend, rise

Mirsab
Wise, prudent

Misbah
A lamp, lantern

Miyar
Respected, high standard

Moazzam
Exalted, respectable

**Mobeen
see Mubeen**

Moeen
Assistant, helper

**Mohammad
see Muhammad**

**Mohammed
see Muhammad**

**Mohsin
see Muhsin**

Mohtaram
Respected, elevated

Moin see Moeen

Momin see Mumin

Moomin
see Mumin

Moonis
Friend, companion

Muadh
Protected

Muallam
Teacher, tutor

Muammar
*Eternal, to live for a
long time, renovator,
architect, matured,
admired*

Muawiyah
*A young warrior, a
gallant young man*

Muawwin
Helper

Muayad
Supported

Muayyad
see Muayad

Muazzam
Respected

Mubarak
see Mubaraq

Mubaraq
Blessed, fortunate

Mubashir
*One who spreads good
news, one of the
attributes of the Prophet
Muhammad*

Mubashshir
see Mubashir

Mubdi
Originator

Mubeen
see Mubin

Mubin
*Evident, clear to see, one
of the attributes of the
Prophet Muhammad*

Mudabbir
Planner

Muddathir
Covered

Mudhakkir
*Reminder, one of the
attributes of the Prophet
Muhammad*

Mueen
Helper

Mufassair
*One who explains,
interpreter*

**Mufeed
see Mufid**

Mufid
Beneficial, useful

Muflih
Successful

Mufti
Religious teacher

**Mugheeth
see Mughith**

Mughith
Helper, assistant

**Mughnee
see Mughni**

Mughni
*One who frees
another from distress,
to enrich*

Muhaddith
Interpreter, explainer

Muhaimin
*One who provides
sanctuary*

Muhammad
*The praised one, the
name of the Prophet*

Muhannad
Sword, scimitar

Muharram
*Sacred, first month of the
Islamic calendar, one of
the attributes of the
Prophet Muhammad*

**Muhaymin
see Muhaimin**

Muhib
Friend

Muhsin
Charitable

Muhtadi
Guided towards the truth

**Muhyee
see Muhyi**

Muhyi
To give life, restore

Muid
Repeat, reproduce

Muin
Helper

Muizz
One who bestows honour

Mujahid
Holy warrior, family

Mujeeb
see Mujib

Mujeer see Mujir

Mujib
To accept, to grant

Mujir
Guardian, protector

Mujtaba
Chosen, one of the attributes of the Prophet Muhammad

Mukammal
Complete

Mukarram
Venerable, one of the attributes of the Prophet Muhammad

Mukhlis
Truthful, sincere, faithful

Mukhtar
To act with a free will, chosen, most exquisite

Mukhtiar
Having authority

Mumin
One who advocates peace and harmony, believer

Mumtaz
Excellent, distinguished

Munaib
On behalf of another

Munaj
Saviour, one of the attributes of the Prophet Muhammad

Munawwar
Illuminated, enlightened

Mundhir
One who warns others of danger

Muneeb
see Munib

Muneem
see Munim

Muneer see Munir

Munib
One who turns to Allah for help

Munim
Generous

Munir
*Bright, shining,
one of the attributes
of the Prophet
Muhammad*

Munis
Companion

Munsif
Judge, arbitrator

Muntaqim
Avenger

Muntasir
*Victorious,
winner*

Muqaddas
Holy

**Muqeet
see Muqit**

Muqit
Provider

Muqsit
Impartial, fair

Muqtadir
Powerful, mighty

Muqtasid
*Intelligent, wise, one of
the attributes of the
Prophet Muhammad*

Murad
Desire, intention

Mureed see Murid

Murid
Follower, disciple

Murih
*Soothing, restful,
comfortable*

Murshid
Teacher, guide

Mursil
Representative, envoy

**Murtada
see Murtadha**

Murtadh
Disciplined, pious

Murtadha
*Accessible, one of the
attributes of the Prophet
Muhammad*

Murtadi
Satisfied, content

Murtah
Content, tranquil,
comfortable

Murtaza
see Murtadha

Musad
Lucky, fortunate

Musaddaq
see Musaddiq

Musaddiq
Believer, one of the
attributes of the Prophet
Muhammad

Musalih
Mediator,
peacemaker

Musawwir
Artist, painter

Musharraf
Honoured, respected

Mushtaq
Desirous, to yearn for

Muslih
Reformer

Mussaddiq
see Musaddiq

Mussarat
Happiness, delight

Mustafa
The chosen one,
one of the attributes
of the Prophet
Muhammad

Mustafeedh
To profit from,
over-flowing river

Mustapha
see Mustafa

Mustaq
see Mushtaq

Muta
Obedient

Mutahar
Pure, immaculate,
without sin, one of the
attributes of Prophet
Muhammad

Mutaher
see Mutahar

Mutahhar
see Mutahar

Mutal
Exalted, rich

Mutaqaddim
Advanced, forward

Mutasim
*Adhering to the faith,
protected*

Mutawakil
Trust in Allah

Mutazz
Proud, mighty

**Mutee
see Muti**

Muti
*Obedient, one of the
attributes of the Prophet
Muhammad*

Mutlaq
Absolute

Mutlu
*Happy,
fortunate*

Muttaqi
Pious, holy

Muwaffaq
Successful

Muwahhid
Desirable

Muzaffar
Victorious

Muzakir
*Reminiscent, evocative,
one of the attributes of
the Prophet Muhammad*

Muzzamil
Covered

Nabeel see Nabil

Nabhan
Aware, attentive, to know what one is doing

Nabih see Nabhan

Nabil
An archer, dextrous

**Nadeem
see Nadim**

Nadeer see Nadir

Nadhir see Nazir

Nadim
Companion

Nadir
Unique, rare, precious

Nadr
Gold

Naeem see Naim

Nafees see Nafis

Nafi
Beneficent, auspicious

Nafis
Pure, refined

Nah
Prohibitor, one of the attributes of the Prophet Muhammad

**Naheed
see Nahid**

Nahid
Respected, elevated

Nail
Acquire, earn

Naim
Pleasure

**Naja
see Najah**

Najah
Secure, safe

Najam
A star, planet

Najee see Naji

**Najeeb
see Najib**

Naji
Safe, confident, one of the attributes of the Prophet Muhammad

Najib
Nobel, generous

Najih
Successful

Najm
see Najam

Namir
Leopard

Naqad
Critic

Naqash
Engraver, artist

Naqeeb
see Naqib

Naqi
Pure, clear

Naqib
Chief, leader

Naqqad see Naqad

Naqqash
see Naqash

Narmin
Soft

Nasar
Victory, support

Naseef see Nasif

Naseem
see Nasim

Naseer see Nasir

Nasif
Fair, just

Nasih
Clever

Nasik
see Nasiq

Nasim
Cool breeze, fragrant air

Nasiq
Holy, pious, well-ordered

Nasir
Friend, defender

Nasr see Nasar

Nassah
Counsellor

Nathar
Scatter, spread

Naushad
Joy, happiness

Naveed
see Navid

Navid
Good news

Nawab
Deputy

Nawaz
Cherished

Nawazish
Kindness, gratitude

Nawfal
*Generous,
sea, ocean*

Nayab
see Nawab

Nayyar
Brilliant, shining

Naz
Pride

Nazar
Charity, offering

Nazeer see Nazir

Nazheef
Clean, chaste

**Nazheer
see Nazhir**

Nazhim
Songwriter, poet

Nazhir
Alike, equal

Nazih
Pure

Nazim see Nazhim

Nazir
*One who warns others of
danger, one of the
attributes of the Prophet
Muhammad*

Nazoor
Protector

Nazr
Oath, promise

Nazzar
Keen-eyed

**Niamat
see Nimah**

Niaz
Offering, donation

Nidal
Defender

Nimah
Blessing, the comforts of life

Nimat
see Nimah

Nimr see Namir

Nishat
Energy, power

Nithar
Sacrifice

Niyyaz see Niaz

Nizam
System, order, a string of pearls

Noor see Nur

Noorani
Brilliant, shining

Noori see Nuri

Nudrat
Rare

Numan
Soul

Nur
Light

Nurani
Luminous

Nuri
Shining, bright

Nusrat
Support, victory

Qabeel
see Qabil

Qabil
Compatible

Qablan see Qabil

Qadeem
see Qadim

Qadeer see Qadir

Qadi
Judge

Qadim
Ancient, wise

Qadir
Powerful, mighty

Qadum
Intrepid, undaunted,
brave

Qaheer see Qahir

Qahhar
Victorious, dominant

Qahir
Victor

Qaid
Leader, chief

Qaim
Established, noble

Qaiser
Emperor, king

Qaiys
see Qays

Qamar
The moon

Qani
Satisfied,
contented

Qarar
Peace, rest, decisive

Qari
One who recites from the
Quran, reader

Qarib
Near, one of the
attributes of the Prophet
Muhammad

Qaseem
see Qasim

Qasim
To share, one of the attributes of the Prophet Muhammad

Qassem see Qasim

Qatadah
Tree

Qavi see Qawi

Qawee see Qawi

Qawi
Strong, firm

Qays
Measurer (Qays and Layla are the Islamic equivalent of Romeo and Juliet)

Qayser see Qaiser

Qayum
Eternal, ascending, elevated

Qayyoom see Qayum

Qayyoum see Qayum

Qayyum see Qayum

Qiyam see Qayum

Qudamah
Courage, bravery

Quddoos see Quddus

Quddous see Quddus

Quddus
To be adored, holy, pure

Qurban
Sacrifice

Qutamiy
Falcon

Qutb see Qutub

Qutub
The north star, pillar of the community or, literally, the fulcrum around which a mill stone rotates

Rabah
Victor

Rabb
Master, father

Rabbani
Devotee, close to Allah

Rabi
Spring (season)

Rabigh
Pleasing, happy

**Radhee
see Radhi**

Radhi
*Blessed by ones parents,
suitor*

Radi see Radhi

Raees see Rais

Rafa
Compassion, mercy

Rafee see Rafi

**Rafeeq
see Rafiq**

Rafi
Exalted, noble

Rafiq
*Gentle, kind-hearted
friend*

Raghib
Willing

Rahat
Rest

**Raheeb
see Rahib**

**Raheem
see Rahim**

Rahib
Priest, devotee

Rahim
Compassionate

Rahman
Merciful, gracious

Rahmat
Mercy, sympathy

Rai
Shepherd

Raid
Leader, pioneer

Raihan
Comfort, fragrant plant

Rais
Leader, prince, nobleman

Raja
Wishful, desire, hope

Rajab
Seventh month of the Islamic calendar

Rajih
Responsive, clever

Rakin
Respectful, noble

Ramadan
Ninth month of the Islamic calendar, holy month of fasting

Ramiz
Symbol, sign

Raoof see Rauf

Raouf see Rauf

Raqaib see Raqib

Raqeeq see Raqiq

Raqib
Supervisor, guardian, protector

Raqim
Writer, author

Raqiq
Sensitive

Rashad
Integrity, to lead a righteous life

Rasheed see Rashid

Rasheeq see Rashiq

Rashid
Guided to the path of rightousness, pious

Rashiq
Handsome, graceful

Rasikh see Rasiq

Rasiq
Stable, balanced, established

Rasool see Rasul

Rasul
Messenger, one of the attributes of the Prophet Muhammad

Ratib
Arranger, organiser

Rauf
Forgiving, compassionate

**Raushan
see Roshan**

**Rayhan
see Raihan**

Rayyan
Complete

Razam
Lion

Razi see Ridhwan

**Razzak
see Razzaq**

Razzaq
Provider

Refiq
Gentle, kind, friend

**Rehmat
see Rahmat**

Riaz see Riyadh

Rida see Ridha

Ridha
Satisfaction, pleasure

Ridhwan
Happiness

**Ridwan
see Ridhwan**

Rifaqat
Companionship

Rifat
Dignity, eminence

Riffat see Rifat

Riyad see Riyadh

Riyadh
Gardens

Riza see Ridha

**Rizwan
see Ridhwan**

Roshan
Illuminated, light

Ruhani
From the soul, spiritual

Ruhi see Ruhani

Rustam
Brave, strong

Sabah
Morning

Sabbar see Sabir

**Sabeeh
see Sabih**

Sabih
*Handsome, fair
complexion*

Sabiq
Preceding

Sabir
*One who endures all
hardships*

Sabooh
Radiant, bright

Saboor see Sabur

Sabour see Sabur

Sabur
*Patient, tolerant, one
who overlooks the faults
of others*

Sad
Prosperity

Sadaqat
Sincerity, truthfulness

Sadat
Happiness, good fortune

Saddeeq
see Sadiq

Saddiq see Sadiq

Sadeed
see Sadid

Sadid
True, correct, straight

Sadik see Sadiq

Sadiq
Honest, a man who keeps his word, one of the attributes of the Prophet Muhammad

Sadr
The highest

Saeed see Said

Safar
Second month of the Islamic calendar

Safdar
Warrior

Safee see Safiy

Safeer
see Safir

Safi see Safiy

Safir
Ambassador, representative

Safiy
Righteous, one of the attributes of the Prophet Muhammad

Safwan
A clear day

Sagh
Listener

Sagheer
see Saghir

Saghir
Small, young

Saheer
see Sahir

Sahib
Companion

Sahir
Awaken

Sahl
Content

Said
Fortunate, venerable

Saif
Sword

Sajad see Sajid

Sajid
Worshipper

Sajjad see Sajid

Sakhawat
Generosity

Sakhi
Liberal, generous

Sakhr
Rock

Salah
Righteousness

Salam
Peace, salvation

Salamah
Safety, well-being

Salamat
see Salamah

Salbih
Handsome, attractive

Saleel
see Salil

Saleem
see Salim

Saleh see Salih

Salih
Virtuous

Salik see Saliq

Salil
Descendant, follower

Salim
Perfect, complete, healthy

Saliq
Follower

Salman
*Affable, of calm
temperement*

Samad
Eternal, perfect

Samee see Sami

Sameem
see Samim

Sameer
see Samir

Sami
All-hearing, all-knowing

Samie see Sami

Samim
Genuine, pure

Samir
Story-teller

Saood
see Saud

Saqar
Eagle

Saqib
Illuminated, dazzling

Saqr see Saqar

Sardar
Leader, commander

Sarfaraz
Respected, honoured

Sarfraz
see Sarfaraz

Sarim
Brave, strong

Sariyah
Clouds at night

Sarmad
Eternal, everlasting

Sartaj
Crown, head, the one in charge

Sarvar see Sarwar

Sarwar
Chief, master

Sarwat
Wealth, abundance

Satar
Forgiving

Saud
Luck

Saulat
Dignity, majesty

Sayeed
Master, leader, chief, one of the attributes of the Prophet Muhammad

Sayyid see Sayeed

Seham
Arrows

Sen
Cheerful

Shaban
*Eighth month of the
Islamic calendar*

**Shabbeer
see Shabir**

**Shabeer
see Shabir**

Shabir
*Dignified, handsome,
virtuous*

Shad
Happy, contented

Shadi
Singer

Shafaqat
Compassionate

Shafat
Mediation, advocacy

Shafee see Shafi

**Shafeeq
see Shafiq**

Shafi
*Healer, one of the
attributes of the Prophet
Muhammad*

Shafiq
*Kind-hearted,
affectionate*

Shah
Ruler, king

Shahab
*Star, meteor,
a man of experience*

Shahbal
King of the falcons

Shahbaz
Hawk, falcon

**Shaheed
see Shahid**

**Shaheen
see Shahin**

**Shaheer
see Shahir**

Shahid
*Witness, one of
the attributes
of the Prophet
Muhammad*

Shahin
White hawk

Shahir
Famous, renowned, one of the attributes of the Prophet Muhammad

Shahzada
Prince

Shaida
Martyr

Shaikh
see Sheikh

Shajee see Shaji

Shaji
Brave, bold, fearless

Shakeel
see Shakil

Shakil
Handsome

Shakir
Grateful, contented

Shakoor
see Shakir

Shakur
see Shakir

Shameem
see Shamim

Shamil
Comprehensive

Shamim
Scented, fragrant air, breeze

Shamis
Sunny

Shams
The sun

Shamshaid
Pine tree

Shamsheer
see Shamshir

Shamshir
Sword, scimitar

Shani
One who cures illnesses

Sharaf
Dignity

Sharafat
see Sharaf

Shareef
see Sharif

Sharf
Honour, esteem

Sharif
Distinguished, noble

Sharik
Companion, partner

Shaukat
Authority, dignity, grandeur

Shauket
see Shaukat

Shauq
Desire, zeal, aspiration, yearning

Shawwal
Tenth month of the Islamic calendar

Sheikh
Leader, a man of experience

Shemissa
Star

Shibl
Lion cub

Shihab
Flame, shooting star

Shir
see Shirzad

Shirzad
Lion

Shua
Sunshine

Shuja
Bold, fearless

Shujat
Bravery, valour

Shukr
see Shakir

Shukri
Thankful

Sibt
Tribe, clan

Siddeeq see Sadiq

Siddiq see Sadiq

Sidq
Truth

Silah
Armour, weapons

Simsek
Lightning

Sinan
Spear heads

Siraj
The sun, lamp, one of the attributes of the Prophet Muhammad

Sirhan
Day dreamer

Sohail
see Suhail

Sohrab
Strong

Soofi see Sufi

Subbooh
Pure, like the morning

Subhan
Divine, holy

Subhi
Early morning

Sufi
Mystic

Sufyan
Chosen one

Suhaib
Red-haired

Suhail
Star

Suhayb
see Suhaib

Suhayl see Suhail

Suhayr
Night

Sulaf
Best

Sultan
King, power

Surur
Happiness, joy

Suud
Good luck

Syed see Sayeed

T

Tabarak
see Tabaraq

Tabaraq
Blessed

Tabassum
Smile

Tabish
Heat, warmth

Tafaddal
Obligation,
welcome

Tahir
Pure, genuine

Tahmeez
see Tahmiz

Tahmiz
Moral, well-mannered

Tahreer
see Tahrir

Tahrir
Liberation

Tahseen
see Tahsin

Tahsin
Make better, improve

Taib
Forgiven

Taj
Crown

Tajammal
see Tajammul

Tajammul
To beautify oneself, to be
adorned

Tajwar
Crowned

Talal
Fine, admirable

Talat
To appear

Talib
A seeker of knowledge

Tameem
Strong, fully grown

Tameez
Discretion, judgement

Tamir
Fruitful

Tamkeen
Majesty, power

Tammam
Complete, good, well done

Tanweer
see Tanwir

Tanwir
Ripen, bloom, the morning light

Tanzil
Inspirational, influential

Taqee see Taqi

Taqi
Devout, pious

Tareef see Tarif

Tarif
Rare, uncommon, special

Tariq
The morning star, night-traveller

Tarlan
Hawk

Tasaddiq
see Tasadduq

Tasadduq
Gift, sacrifice

Tasawar
Imagination

Tasleem
see Taslim

Taslim
Acceptance, submission

Tatheer
see Tahthir

Tathir
Impression

Taufiq
Divine guidance

Tawaddud
Befriending, love

Tawfeeq
see Taufiq

Tawfiq
see Taufiq

Tawqeer
see Tawqir

Tawqir
*Respect, honour,
reverence*

Tawwab
Forgiving, relenting

Tayab see Tayib

Tayib
*Good, one of the
attributes of the Prophet
Muhammad*

Taymullah
Servant of Allah

**Tayseer
see Taysir**

Taysir
To make easy

Tayyib see Tayib

Thabit
Well established, brave

Thalab
Fox

**Thamar
see Thamir**

Thamir
Profitable, fruitful

Thana
Praise, glorification

Thaqib
*Shining brightly,
splendid*

Tharwat
Wealth, power, influence

Thaur
Bull

Thurayya
Star

Timsah
Crocodile

Tufail
Mediator

Tufayl see Tufail

Turab
Soil, sand, dust

Ubadah
*Prayer,
worshipping*

Ubaid
Servant

**Ubayd
see Ubaid**

**Ubaydah
see Ubaid**

Ufuq
Horizon

Ugur
Good luck

Ulfat
Friendship, love

Umar also Omar
The first son

Umarah
Architect

Umayr
Small

Umid
Hope

Umran
Prosperity

Unais
*Affection, love, friend,
companion*

**Unays
see Unais**

Uqab
Eagle

Uqbah
Final

Urooq
Zenith, ascend

Urwah
Support

Usaid
Young lion

**Usama
see Usamah**

Usamah
Lion

**Usayd
see Usaid**

Utbah
Step

Uzam
Greatest, most pious

Wadad see Wadud

Wadi
Calm, peaceful

**Wadood
see Wadud**

Wadud
*Beloved friend,
companion*

Wafeeq see Wafiq

Wafi
Loyal, faithful

Wafiq
*Successful, victorious,
winner*

Wahab
Gift, charity

Waheed see Wahid

Wahaj
Shining, radiant

Waheeb see Wahib

Wahib
Provider

Wahid
Unique

Wail
Refuge

Waiz
Preacher

Wajahah
Dignity

**Wajahat
see Wajahah**

**Wajeeh
see Wajih**

Wajid
One who endeavours

Wajih
Of good appearance

**Wakeel
see Wakil**

Wakil
Counsellor

Waleed see Walid

Walee see Wali

Wali
Prince, defender

Walid
Boy

Waliy see Wali

Wamiq
Loving, affectionate

Waqar
Integrity, modesty

Waris
Successor, heir

Warith see Waris

Wasee see Wasi

Waseel see Wasil

**Waseem
see Wasim**

Waseer see Wazir

Wasi
Plenty, all embracing

Wasif
Servant, assistant

Wasil
Friendship, partnership

Wasim
Handsome

Wasir see Wazir

Wathiq
Close, confident, firm

Wazeer see Wazir

Wazir
Adviser, helping hand

Wilaiyat
Power, authority

Wirasat
Inheritance

**Wirathat
see Wirasat**

Yagmur
Rain

**Yameen
see Yamin**

Yamin
Auspicious, blessed

**Yaqoob
see Yaqub**

Yaqoot
Precious stone

Yaqub
Beautiful bird

Yar
Friend, companion

Yasar
*Ease, wealth,
prosperity*

Yasir
Simple, easy

Yawar
Aide, assistant

Yazdan
To beautify, to look good

Yazeed see Yazid

Yazid
Increasing, multiplying

Yener
Vanquishing

Yildirim
Lightning

Yildiz
Stars

Yoonus see Younis

Yoosuf see Yusuf

Younis
Companion or, literally, to keep you company

Yousuf see Yusuf

Yumn
Happiness, wealth

Yunus see Younis

Yusuf
Handsome

Z

Zafar
Victory, triumph

Zafeer see Zafir

Zafir
Firm, resolute

**Zaheer
see Zahir**

Zahid
Devotee, self-denying

Zahir
Shining, flower in bloom

Zaid see Ziyad

Zaim
Chief, leader

Zain see Zayn

Zaiyan
Good-looking

Zaka
Keen perception, sharpness of mind

Zakee see Zaki

Zaki
Intelligent, virtuous

Zakir
One who constantly praises Allah, grateful

Zakiy see Zaki

Zakiyy see Zaki

Zamain
Guarantor, sponsor

Zaman
Time

Zamanat
Guarantee

Zameer see Zamir

Zamir
Conscience

Zareef see Zarif

Zarif
Witty, jovial

Zauq
Taste

Zayd see Ziyad

Zayir
Guest, visitor

Zayn
Honour, ornament, to adorn

**Zayyan
see Zaiyan**

Zia
Brilliance, splendour

Zirgham
Lion, brave, mighty

Ziyad
Plenty

Zoka
The sun, dawn

Zubair
A brave and wise man

**Zubayr
see Zibair**

Zufar
Brave, like a lion

**Zuhair
see Zahir**

Zuhayr
Flowering, bright

Zuhoor
Arising, appearing

Zulfaqar
The sword of the Prophet Muhammad

Zulfiqar
see Zulfaqar

The Modern Book of Muslim Names

Girls

Abdah
Servant

Abeer see Abir

Abida see Abidah

Abidah
Worshipper, devotee

Abir
Fragrance, perfume, aroma

Ablah
Perfectly formed

Abqara see Abqarah

Abqarah
Beautiful, delicate

Adara see Azra

Adeeba see Adibah

Adibah
Writer, intellectual

Adila see Adilah

Adilah
Righteous, just

Afaf
Chastity, purity, modesty

Afeefa see Afifah

Afeefah see Afifah

Afifa see Afifah

Afifah
Modest, chaste, decent

Afiyah
Fitness, health, vigour

Afra
Fair complexion

Afreeda see Afridah

Afridah
Creative

Afrodha see Afrozah

Afroz
Enlightening

Afroza
see Afrozah

Afrozah
Turquoise

Afsah see Afzah

Afzah
Enlarging, growing

Ahd
Pledge, word of honour

Ahlam
Utopia, perfection,
dreams

Aida see Aidah

Aidah
Returning

Aisha see Aishah

Aishah
Prosperous, happy,
fortunate, the name of
the wife of the Prophet
Muhammad

Aiysha
see Aishah

Akeeda
see Akidah

Akida see Akidah

Akidah
Certain, firm, resolute

Akifa see Akifah

Akifah
To worship Allah in
solitude

Alamira
Princess

Aleema
see Alimah

Aleeyah
see Aliyah

Alia see Aliyah

Alima
see Alimah

Alimah
Educated, learned, skilled
in music and dance

Aliyah
Exalted, highest social
standing, elevated

Aliyyah see Aliyah

Alliyya see Aliyah

Almas
Diamond, precious

Almeira
see Almira

Almira
Truth without question

Almirah
see Almira

Altair
Bird

Alula
The first

Alzena
Woman, the embodiment of all feminine charm and virtue

Amaima
see Amaymah

Amal
Hope, aspiration, desire

Amani
Wishes, aspirations

Amarah
Tolerant

Amatullah
Servant of Allah

Amaymah
Tall, beautiful

Ambar
Perfume, ambergris

Ambreen
see Ambrin

Ambrin
Ambergris

Ameena
see Aminah

Ameenah
see Aminah

Ameera
see Amirah

Amila see Amilah

Amilah
Wishful, hopeful

Amina
see Aminah

Aminah
Trustworthy, a woman who advocates peace and harmony

Amira see Amirah

Amirah
Princess

**Amtullah
see Amatullah**

Anah
Patience, perseverance

Anan
The sky

Anbar see Ambar

**Anbreen
see Ambrin**

Andalah
Song of the nightingale

**Andaleeb
see Andalib**

Andalib
Nightingale

**Andleeb
see Andalib**

**Aneeqa
see Aniqah**

**Aneesa
see Anisah**

Aniqah
Beautiful, graceful

Anisa see Anisah

Anisah
*Good natured,
affectionate, friend*

Anjum
Stars

Anwar
Ray of light

Aqeela see Aqilah

**Aqeelah
see Aqilah**

Aqila see Aqilah

Aqilah
Sensible, wise, intelligent

Arah
Adoring

**Areeba
see Aribah**

Areefa see Arifah

Areej see Arij

Arejah see Arijah

Ariba see Aribah

Aribah
Wise, literary

Arifa see Arifah

Arifah
Expert, one who possesses knowledge of Allah and his kingdom

Arij
Fragrance

Arijah
Fragrant, aromatic

Arub
Loving, affectionate

Aselah see Asilah

Asilah
Genuine, authentic, original

Asimah
Safe, virtuous

Asira see Asirah

Asirah
Bonded

Asiyah
Strong, supportive

Asiyya see Asiyah

Asma
Precious

Asyma see Asimah

Ateeka see Atiqah

Atifa see Atifah

Atifah
Compassionate, sympathetic

Atika see Atiqah

Atikah see Atiqah

Atiqah
Mature

Atira see Atirah

Atirah
Aromatic, fragrant

Atiyah
Gift, reward

Atiyyah see Atiyah

Attia see Atiyah

Attiya see Atiyah

**Attofa
see Attufah**

Attufah
Kind, compassionate

Atun
Teacher

Awabah
Guided

Awatif
Sentiments, emotions

**Ayesha
see Aishah**

**Azeema
see Azimah**

**Azeemah
see Azimah**

**Azeeza
see Azizah**

**Azeezah
see Azizah**

Azhar
Flowers, blossom

Azimah
Great, dignified

Aziza see Azizah

Azizah
Esteemed, cherished

Azra see Azrah

Azrah
Maiden, pearl

Azza see Azzah

Azzah
Gazelle

Badihah
Insight, perception

Badr
The full moon

Badria
see Badriyah

Badriyah
Early bird, the light of the full moon, beautiful

Badriyya
see Badriyah

Badriyyah
see Badriyah

Bahar
Spring (season)

Bahij
Splendid, magnificent

Bahira
see Bahirah

Bahirah
Moonlight, brilliance

Bahiyah
Beautiful, radiant

Bahiyya
see Bahiyah

Bahiyyah
see Bahiyah

Bahjat
Radiant

Baigum
Woman, lady, wife

Bakara
see Bakarah

Bakarah
Purity

Bakht
Luck, fortune

Bakurah
First, achievement

Baleegha
see Balighah

Balighah
Everlasting, eloquent

Banan
Finger tips

Bareah see Bariah

Bariah
Innocent, angel

Baseema
see Basimah

Baseer see Basir

Basheera
see Bashirah

Basheerah
see Bashirah

Bashira
see Bashirah

Bashirah
*The bringer of glad
tidings*

Basila see Basilah

Basilah
Daring, brave, fearless

Basimah
Smiling, happy, joyful

Basir
Perception, forsight

Basma
see Basmah

Basmah
Smile

Batool
see Batul

Batul
Chaste, pure

Bettula
Maiden, young girl

Bibi
Lady

Bilqees
see Bilqis

Bilqis
*The name of the
Queen of Sheba*

Bint
Daughter of

Bossaina
see Buthaynah

Bulbul
Nightingale

Bushra
see Bushrah

Bushrah
Good news, glad tidings

Buthaina
see Buthaynah

Buthaynah
Beautiful

Dalal
Pampered

Deeba see Dibah

Delilah
Guide, leader

Dhakiyah
Intelligent, bright

Dibah
Golden

Dilaram
Peace of mind

Dilshad
Heart-warming

Duha
Morning, brightness

Durdana
Pearl, gem stone

Durrah
Precious pearl

Fadheelah
see Fadilah

Fadilah
Accomplished,
perfection

Fadwa
see Fadwah

Fadwah
Thoughtful, unselfish

Faghira
Jasmine

Faheema
see Fahima

Faheemah
see Fahimah

Fahima
see Fahimah

Fahimah
Intelligent

Fahmeeda
see Fahmidah

Fahmida
see Fahmidah

Fahmidah
Intelligent, wise

Faidah
Advantage, rewarding,
benefit

Faidha
see Faidah

Faiqa
see Faiqah

Faiqah
Best, superb, excellent

Fairoza
Turquoise

Faizah
Victorious, successful

Fakhira
see Fakhirah

Fakhirah
Precious

Fakhiriyah
see Fakhriyah

Fakhriya
see Fakhriyah

Fakhriyah
Pride, integrity, glory

Faqihah
Expert, understanding, knowledgeable

Farah
Happiness, joy

Fareeda
see Faridah

Fareedah
see Faridah

Farhana
see Farhanah

Farhanah
Happy, joyful

Farhat
Delight, pleasure

Faria
Beautiful, pretty

Farida
see Faridah

Faridah
Unique, precious

Fariha
see Farihah

Farihah
Happy, joyful, lively, content

Farwah
Fur

Farzana
see Farzanah

Farzanah
Wise, clever, one who makes the right choice

Faseeha
see Fasihah

Fasihah
Educated, literary, eloquent

Fataina
see Fatan

Fatan
Wise, intelligent

Fatima
see Fatimah

Fatimah
Baby girl

Fatin
see Fatinah

Fatinah
Charming, enchanting, beautiful

Fatoona
see Fatunah

Fatunah
Alert

Faudhia
see Fawziyah

Fauzah
Triumph

Fauzia
see Fawziyah

Fawhah
Aroma, fragrance

Fawzah
see Fauzah

Fawziyah
Successful, victorious

Fawziyyah
see Fawziyah

Fayadhah
Generous, bountiful

Fayruz
Turquoise

Fazeelat
see Fazilat

Fazilat
Virtue, good deed

Firdaus
see Firdaws

Firdaws
Paradise, bed of roses

Firdows
see Firdaws

Furkhanda
Happy, joyful

Gauhar
Gem, pearl

Ghada
see Ghadah

Ghadah
Beautiful, pretty

Ghaliya
see Ghaliyah

Ghaliyah
Dear, beloved

Ghayda
see Ghaydah

Ghaydah
Young,
delicate

Ghazala
see Ghazalah

Ghazalah
The sun, gazelle

Ghaziya
see Ghaziyah

Ghaziyah
Warrior

Ghusoon
see Ghusun

Ghusun
Branch

Gul
Flower, blossom

Gulab
Rose

Gulshan
Garden

Gulzar
see Gulshan

Hebeeba
see Habibah

Habeebah
see Habibah

Habiba
see Habibah

Habibah
Beloved

Hadiya
see Hadiyah

Hadiyah
Guided to the truth,
calm, tranquil, gift

Hadiyya
see Hadiyah

Hadiyyah
see Hadiyah

Hafeeza
see Hafizah

Hafeezah
see Hafizah

Hafizah
Guardian, protector

Hafsa see Hafsah

Hafsah
Lion cub

Hajar
Migrant, wanderer

Hajira see Hajirah

Hajirah
Nomad

Hakimah
Moonlight, wise, just

Halah
Halo

Haleema
see Halimah

Haleemah
see Halimah

Halimah
Patient, to persevere

Hamaiza
Joyful, jovial

Hameeda
see Hamidah

Hameedah
see Hamidah

Hameema
see Hamimah

Hamida
see Hamidah

Hamidah
Praiseworthy, one who praises and glorifies Allah

Hamimah
Close friend, companion

Hammada
see Hammadah

Hammadah
Praising Allah

Hana see Hannah

Hanna see Hannah

Hanan see Hannan

Haneefa
see Hanifah

Haneefah
see Hanifah

Haneen see Hanin

Haniah
see Haniyah

Hanifa
see Hanifah

Hanifah
Follower of the truth

Hanin
Yearning, longing, desiring

Haniyah
Contented

Haniyya
see Haniyah

Haniyyah
see Haniyah

Hanna
see Hannah

Hannah
Happiness, bliss

Hannan
Affectionate, tender, mercy

Hareer see Harir

Harir
Silk

Harisah
Protector, guardian

Harithah
Lioness

**Haseefah
see Hasifah**

**Haseena
see Hasinah**

**Haseenah
see Hasinah**

**Hasefah
see Hasifah**

Hasifah
*One with sound
judgement, clever, wise*

Hasinah
Well protected, beautiful

Hasna
Beautiful, pious

Hassanah
Beautiful, pious

Hawwa
Beautiful

Haya
Modesty, shyness

Hayah
Life, living

Hayat see Hayah

Hayfa
Slender, beautiful

Hibah
Gift, present, reward

Hikmah
Prudence, wisdom

Hoor see Hur

Huda
Guided to the truth

**Humaira
see Humayra**

Humayra
Of reddish complexion

Hur
Angels, young

**Hurairah
see Hurayrah**

Hurayrah
Kitten

Huriyah
Freedom, liberty

**Huriyyah
see Huriyah**

**Hurriyah
see Huriyah**

Husn
Beauty

Husna
The most beautiful

I

Ibreez see Ibriz

Ibrisam
Silk

Ibriz
Gold, precious

Ibtehaj see Ibtihaj

**Ibtesam
see Ibtisam**

Ibtihaj
Joy, delight, happiness

Ibtihal
Prayer

Ibtisam
Smile

Iffah see Iffat

Iffat
*Purity, chastity, virtue,
modesty*

Ikram
Honour, generosity

Ilham
Intuition, inspiration

Iman
Faith, belief

Imtithal
*Acceptance,
obedience*

Inam
Act of kindness

Inas
Sociable

Inayah
Concern, attention

Inayat see Inayah

Intisar
Triumph, victory

Iram
Heaven, paradise

Isha see Aishah

Ismat
*Honour, protection,
chastity*

Izdihar
*Flourishing, blossoming,
prosperity*

J

Jala
Clarity, purity

Jalala
Glorious

**Jaleela
see Jalilah**

Jalila see Jalilah

Jalilah
Splendid, fine

**Jameela
see Jamilah**

**Jameelah
see Jamilah**

**Jamila
see Jamilah**

Jamilah
Beautiful, graceful

Janan
Soul

Janat see Janan

Jannah
Heaven,
paradise

Jasmeen
see Yasmin

Jasmin
see Yasmin

Jasmine
see Yasmin

Jauhara
see Jawharah

Jawaheer
see Jawahir

Jawahir
Jewels

Jawharah
Jewel

Jeelan
Gazelle

Jehan
The world

Jena
Little bird

Jumanah
Pearl

Junaynah
Garden

Juneena
see Junaynah

Juwairiyyah
see Juwayriyah

Juwayriyah
Maiden

Kabeera
see **Kabirah**

Kabira
see **Kabirah**

Kabirah
Great, large

Kaleema
see **Kalimah**

Kalila see Kalilah

Kalilah
Beloved

Kalima
see **Kalimah**

Kalimah
Word

Kamilah
Perfect, complete

Kaneez see Kaniz

Kaniz
Servant, attendant

Kanwal
Water lily

Karam
Generosity

Kareema
see **Karimah**

Kareemah
see **Karimah**

Karima
see **Karimah**

Karimah
Generous, invaluable

Karm
Fig trees

Kashifa
see **Kashfah**

Kashifah
Discoverer

Kauser
*Fountain, river in
Paradise*

Kauthar
see **Kauser**

Kawthar
see **Kauser**

Khadeeja
see Khadijah

Khadeejah
see Khadijah

Khadijah
Girl, daughter

Khairun
Best, the most beautiful

Khaleela
see Khalilah

Khaleeqa
see Khaliqa

Khalida
see Khalidah

Khalidah
Immortal, eternal

Khalilah
Friend,
companion

Khaliqa
Well-mannered, able

Khalisah
Pure, clear

Khanam
Lady

Khariya
see Khayriyah

Khateeba
see Khatibah

Khatibah
Speaker, orator

Khatoon
see Khatun

Khatun
Lady, woman

Khawala
Dancer

Khawlah
Deer

Khayriyah
Charitable,
good

Khayriyyah
see Khayriyah

Khulood
see Khulud

Khulud
Immortality

Khuzamah
Lavender

Kubra see Kubrah

Kubrah
Great

**Kulsoom
see Kulthum**

**Kulthoom
see Kulthum**

Kulthum
Healthy

L

**Labeeba
see Labibah**

Labibah
Quick, intelligent, wise

**Laeeqa
see Laiqah**

Laila see Laylah

Laiqah
Deserving, worthy

**Lamees
see Lamisah**

**Lamis
see Lamisah**

Lamisah
Soft, delicate

**Lateefa
see Latifah**

**Lateefah
see Latifah**

Latifa see Latifah

Latifah
Gracious, elegant, agreeable

Layinah
Supple, tender

Layla see Laylah

Laylah
Dark-haired one, beloved

Layyinah
see Layinah

Leena see Lina

Leila
see Laylah

Leilah
see Laylah

Letifa
see Latifah

Lilah see Laylah

Lina
Tender, delicate

Loulou
Pearl, gem

Lubabah
Essential, vital

Lubna
Sweet, sweeter than honey

Lutfiya
see Lutfiyah

Lutfiyah
Graceful, delicate, kind

Lutfiyya
see Lutfiya

Madaniya
see Madaniyah

Madaniyah
Cultured

Madeeha
see Madihah

Madihah
Praiseworthy,
commendable

Mafooza
see Mahfuzah

Mah
The moon

Maha
Very beautiful, graceful

Mahbooba
see Mahbubah

Mabubah
Beloved

Mahdiyah
Guided to the truth

Mahdiyyah
see Mahdiyah

Mahfuzah
Protected,
secure

Mahjabeen
see Mahjabin

Mahjabin
Like the moon

Mahmooda
see Mahmudah

Mahmoodah
see Mahmudah

Mahmouda
see Mahmudah

Mahmudah
Praiseworthy

Maimoona
see Maymunah

Maimoonah
see Maymunah

Maisa
see Maysah

Maisah
see Maysah

Maisun
see Maysun

Majdah
Glory

Majdiyah
Glorious

Majeeda
see Majidah

Majeedah
see Majidah

Majida
see Majidah

Majidah
Glorious,
honourable

Makarim
Gifts, of good character

Makhduma
Served, looked after

Malak
Angel

Malaka
see Malikah

Maleehah
see Malilah

Malihah
Beautiful,
charming

Malika
see Malikah

Malikah
Queen, reigning

Mamoona
see Mamuna

Mamuna
Protected, trustworthy,
safe

Manal
Achievement

Manar
Guiding light, guided to
the right path

Mansurah
Supported,
victorious

Maqsooda
see Maqsuda

Maqsouda
see Maqsuda

Maqsuda
Objective

Maram
Desire, aspiration

Mardiyah
Pleasing

Marghubah
Desired

Mariha
see **Marihah**

Marihah
Lively, cheerful

Mariyah
Fair complexion

Marmarin
Like marble

Marufa
see **Marufah**

Marufah
Accepted, renowned, benefit

Marwareed
see **Marwarid**

Marwarid
Pearl, gem

Mashhoodah
see **Mashudah**

Mashudah
Present, visible

Masooda
see **Masudah**

Masoodah
see **Musadah**

Masooma
see **Masumah**

Masoomah
see **Masumah**

Masouda
see **Masudah**

Masroora
see **Masrurah**

Masrurah
Happy, delighted, joyful

Mastoora
see **Masturah**

Masturah
Hidden, secret

Masudah
Happy, fortunate

Masuma
see **Masumah**

Masumah
Innocent

Mateenah
see Matinah

Matinah
Of resolute mind, strong

Mawahib
Talented

Mawiyah
*Shielded,
protected*

Mayadah
Proud

Maymunah
Blessed, fortunate

Maysa
see Maysah

Maysah
Upright, proud

Maysun
Beautiful face

Mayyada
see Mayadah

Mayyadah
see Mayadah

Maziyah
Virtue, merit, excellence

Moonisah
see Munisah

Muazzamah
Great, respected, exalted

Mubaraka
see Mubarakah

Mubarakah
Blessed

Mubeena
see Mubinah

Mubeenah
see Mubinah

Mubinah
Clear, evident

Mufeeda
see Mufidah

Mufidah
*Useful, helpful,
favourable*

Muhjah
Lifeblood, heart, soul, life

Muhsana
see Muhsanah

Muhsanah
Protected, safe, secure

Muhsina
see Muhsinah

Muhsinah
Benevolent, charitable

Mujahida
see Mujahidah

Mujahidah
Warrior

Mujeeba
see Mujibah

Mujeebah
see Mujibah

Mujiba
see Mujibah

Mujibah
To answer, grant

Mukarramah
Honoured, revered

Mukhlisah
Faithful, pure-hearted, devoted

Muminah
A believer, one who bestows peace and harmony

Mumtaz
Excellent, distinguished

Muna see Munah

Munah
Wish, desire

Munaiba
see Munaybah

Munawara
see Munawarah

Munawarah
Illuminated, brilliant

Munawwar
see Munawarah

Munawwarah
see Munawarah

Munaybah
Guided to the right path

Munazzah
Clean, honest, infallible

Muneebah
see Munibah

Muneera
see Munirah

Muneerah
see Munirah

Munibah
One who turns to Allah
for guidance

Munira
see Munirah

Munirah
Illuminating,
shining

Munisah
Friend,
companion

Munnah
Strength, vigour

Muqaddasa
see Muqaddasah

Muqaddasah
Sacred, holy, pious

Muriha
see Murihah

Murihah
Restful, soothing,
contentment

Murshida
see Murshidah

Murshidah
Guide to the path
of righteousness

Musaddiqa
see Musaddiqah

Musaddiqah
Truthful,
trustworthy

Musahiba
see Musahibah

Musahibah
Companion, friend, ally

Musharrafah
Exalted, honoured,
esteemed

Musharrifa
see Musharrafah

Mushira
see Mushirah

Mushirah
To advise,
to give counsel

Mutahara
see Mutaharah

Mutaharah
Clean, purified, chaste

Mutahharah
see Mutaharah

Nabeeha
see Nabihah

Nabeela
see Nabilah

Nabeelah
see Nabilah

Nabihah
*Eminent, intelligent,
noble, wise*

Nabila
see Nabilah

Nabilah
Respected, beautiful

Nada
Generosity

Nadeeda
see Nadidah

Nadeemah
see Nadimah

Nadheera
see Nadhirah

Nadhirah
Healthy

Nadia
see Nadiyah

Nadidah
Equal

Nadimah
Companion, friend

Nadira
see Nadirah

Nadirah
Precious, rare

Nadiyah
Announcer, caller

Nadrah
*Blooming,
glamorous*

Nadwa
see Nadwah

Nadwah
Dew

Naeema
see Naimah

Naeemah
see Naimah

Nafeesa
see Nafisah

Nafeesah
see Nafisah

Nafiah
Advantageous, good

Nafisah
*Precious, pure,
exquisite*

Nageena
see Naginah

Naghma
see Naghmah

Naghmah
Melody, song

Nagina
see Naginah

Naginah
*Diamond,
precious stone*

Naheed see Nahid

Naheedah
see Nahidah

Nahid
Elevated

Nahidah
Attractive, honourable

Nahlah
Water spring

Nailah
Something worth aquiring

Naima
see Naimah

Naimah
Comfort, pleasure

Nairah
Shining, glittering

Najah
Success

Najat
Safety, security

Najdah
Help

Najeeba
see Najibah

Najeebah
see Najibah

Najeedah
see Najidah

Najia see Najiah

Najiah
Safe, to escape trouble

Najiba
see Najibah

Najibah
Distinguished, praiseworthy

Najidah
Courageous, brave, one who accomplishes difficult tasks

Najiyah
see Najiah

Najiyya
see Najiah

Najla
Wide-eyed, having beautiful eyes

Najma
see Najmah

Najmah
Star

Najwa
Confidential, secret, romantic conversation

Nakhat
*Naturally generous,
fragrant*

Naqeeba
see Naqibah

Naqiba
see Naqibah

Naqibah
Leader

Naqiyah
Clean, clear, pure

Naria
see Nariah

Nariah
Shining

Narjis
The narcissus flower

Naseeba
see Nasibah

Naseeka
see Nasiqa

Naseela
see Nasilah

Naseelah
see Nasilah

Naseemah
see Nasimah

Naseera
see Nasirah

Naseerah
see Nasirah

Nasha
*To awaken with the smell
of pure scent, perfume*

Nashwa
see Nashwah

Nashwah
Fragrance, aroma, elated

Nasia
see Nasihah

Nasiba
see Nasibah

Nasibah
Destiny, fate

Nasifah
Fair, just

Nasihah
Advise, counsel

Nasilah
Honey

Nasima
see Nasimah

Nasimah
Cool breeze,
fragrant air

Nasiqa
Gold

Nasira
see Nasirah

Nasirah
Friend, helper

Nasreen
see Nasrin

Nasrin
White rose

Natharah
Literary

Naufa
see Nawfa

Nawal
Gift

Nawar
Flower, blossom

Nawfa
Excess, abundance

Nayar
Shining, luminous

Nayyar
see Nayar

Naz
see Naziah

Nazahah
Purity, righteousness,
honesty

Nazakat
Neatness

Nazeefah
see Nazifah

Nazeeha
see Nazihah

Nazeera
see Nazirah

Nazeerah
see Nazirah

Nazheera
see Nazhirah

Nazheerah
see Nazhirah

Nazhira
see Nazhirah

Nazhirah
Alike, equal

Nazia
see Naziah

Naziah
Pride

Nazifah
Clean, chaste

Nazihah
*Honest, pure, just,
unspoilt*

Nazira
see Nazirah

Nazirah
*One who warns
others of danger*

Nazneen
see Naznin

Naznin
Delicate

Neelam see Nilam

Neelofar
see Nilofar

Niamat
see Niyamat

Nibal
Arrows

Nida
Call

Nighat
Vision, sight

Nihal
Gifts, presents

Nihla
see Nihlah

Nihlah
Gift, present

Nijiyyah
Useful, helpful

Nikhat
*Sweet smell, aroma,
fragrance, flavour*

Nilam
Pearl-like

Nilofar
Lotus

Nimah
Blessing, comforts of life

Nimat
see Nimah

Nisa
Woman

Nishat
Happiness, joy

Niyamat
Blessing, gift

Noor see Nur

Noora see Nur

Noorun see Nur

Noshaba
Nectar

Nudar
Gold

Nuha
Intelligent

Nur
Light

Nura see Nur

**Nuraniya
see Nuraniyah**

Nuraniyah
Brilliant

Nureen see Nurin

Nurin
Luminous, bright

Nuriyah
Radiant, brilliant

Nurun see Nur

Nusha
Dignity, esteem

**Nusheen
see Nushin**

**Nusheenah
see Nushinah**

Nushin
Sweet

Nushinah
Desirable, lovable

Nusrat
Support, help

Nuzha see Nuzhah

Nuzhah
Fresh, cheerful

**Nuzhat
see Nuzhah**

Qabilah
To accept

Qadira
see Qadirah

Qadirah
Mighty, powerful, able

Qahirah
Triumphant,
victorious

Qaisara
see Qaysarah

Qamar
The moon

Qaysarah
Empress, queen

Quddoosiyyah
see Qudsiyah

Qudisiyya
see Qudsiyah

Qudsiyah
Sacred, blessed

Qudsiyyah
see Qudsiyah

Quratulain
see Qurratulayn

Qurratulayn
The apple of one's eye

R

Rabab
White cloud

Rabeeah
see Rabiah

Rabi
Fragrant breeze,
harvest

Rabiah
Spring, flowering

Radeyah
see Radiyah

Radhia
see Raziah

Radhiyyah
see Radiyah

Radiyah
Contented, happy

Raeesa
see Raisah

Raeesah
see Raisah

Rafa
Happiness, prosperity

Rafeeah
see Rafiah

Rafeeqah
see Rafiqah

Rafia see Rafiah

Rafiah
Sublime, a woman of
honour and nobility

Rafiqa see Rafiqah

Rafiqah
Companion

Raghd
Pleasure, pleasant

Raghibah
Desirous

Rahah
Comfort, rest

Raheel see Rahil

Raheema
see Rahimah

Raheemah
see Rahimah

Rahil
Always on the move, traveller, migrant

Rahima
see Rahimah

Rahimah
Kind, affectionate

Rahmah
Mercy, compassion

Raidah
Pioneer, leader, at the forefront

Raiesa
see Raisah

Raihah
Fragrance, perfume

Raihana
Bouquet of flowers, sweet-smelling flower

Raima see Raimah

Raimah
Tame

Raisah
Princess, Leader

Raiya see Raiyah

Raiyah
Carer

Raja
Hope

Rajeeya
see Rajiyah

Rajiyah
Hopeful, optimistic

Rakeeza
see Rakizah

Rakhshana
Brilliant dawn, illuminated

Rakhshanda
see Rakhshana

Rakizah
Pillar of strength

Ramlah
Sand

Rana
Graceful, beautiful

Rand
Sweet-smelling tree

Rani
Queen

Raniya
see **Raniyah**

Raniyah
Gazing, looking

Raqeema
see **Raqimah**

Raqiah
see **Raqiyah**

Raqibah
Observer

Raqimah
Intelligent, chaste

Raqiyah
Clever, highest

Rasha
Young gazelle

Rasheedah
see **Rashidah**

Rasheeqa
see **Rashiqah**

Rashida
see **Rashidah**

Rashidah
Follower of the path of righteousness, pious

Rashiqah
Graceful, elegant

Rasikhah
Established

Raum
Loving, caring, tender

Rawa see Rawah

Rawah
Fresh air

Rawdah
Garden in Paradise

Rawiyah
Patient

Rayhanah
Basil (herb), aromatic

Rayya
Quenched

Razeena
see **Razinah**

Razia see Raziah

Raziah
Satisfied, contented

Razinah
Respectable, resolute

Reem see Rimah

Reema see Rimah

Rehab
*Gardens, open
countryside*

Rehana
Aromatic, fragrant

Reshman
Soft, smooth, silky

**Ridhwana
see Ridhwanah**

Ridhwanah
Pleasure, contentment

Rifah
Love, harmony

Rifat
Dignity, eminence

Rim see Rimah

Rima see Rimah

Rimah
Antelope, gazelle

**Rizwana
see Ridwanah**

Romana
Loving, romantic

**Roxana
see Rakhshana**

**Roxanna
see Rakhshana**

Rubee see Rubi

Rubi
Gem, precious stone

Ruhaniyah
Spiritual

Ruhee see Ruhi

Ruhi
Spiritual

**Ruhiyah
see Ruhaniyah**

Rukan
Steady, confident

Ruqaiyah
Superior

**Ruqayya
see Ruqaiyah**

**Ruqayyah
see Ruqaiyah**

Rushda
see Rushdiyah

Rushdiyah
Guided to the truth

Ruwa
Pretty

Ruwaidah
see Ruwaydah

Ruwayda
see Ruwaydah

Ruwaydah
Walking gently

S

Saba see Sabah

Sabah
Morning

Sabburah
Enduring, patient

Sabeehah
see Sabihah

Sabeela
see Sabilah

Sabihah
Graceful, beautiful

Sabila see Sabilah

Sabilah
Beautiful, pretty

Sabira
see Sabirah

Sabirah
Patient, enduring

Sabiya
see Sabiyah

Sabiyah
Girl

Saboora
see Sabburah

Sabura
see Sabburah

Saddiqa
see Sadiqah

Sadia see Sadiyah

Sadiqah
Sincere, honest

Sadiyah
Fortunate, blessed

Saeeda
see Saidah

Saeedah
see Saidah

Safa
Sincerity, purity of mind, genuine

Safia see Safiyah

Safiyah
Bountiful or, literally, a palm tree bearing much fruit

Safiyyah
see Safiyah

Sagheera
see Saghirah

Sagheerah
see Saghirah

Saghira
see Saghirah

Saghirah
Small, slender

Sahar
Early morning, dawn, magical

Sahba
Overwhelming

Sahira see Sahirah

Sahirah
The moon

Sahlah
Fluent

Saibah
Direct, one who gets straight to the point

Saidah
Fortunate

Saieda see Saidah

Saim see Saimah

Saimah
Fast, to abstain

Saiqa see Saiqah

Saiqah
Lightning

Saiyidah
Leader

Sajida see Sajidah

Sajidah
*To prostrate oneself
before Allah*

**Sajjida
see Sajidah**

**Sakeena
see Sakinah**

**Sakeenah
see Sakinah**

**Sakina
see Sakinah**

Sakinah
*Peace of mind,
tranquility*

Salamah
Peace, salvation

**Saleema
see Salimah**

**Saleemah
see Salimah**

**Saleha
see Salihah**

Saliha see Salihah

Salihah
Devout, virtuous

**Salima
see Salimah**

Salimah
Healthy, protected

Salma see Salmah

Salmah
*To obey, to bow one's
head in submission*

Salwa see Salwah

Salwah
Solace, comfort

Samah
Forgiveness

Samar
Company

**Sameeha
see Samihah**

**Sameema
see Samimah**

**Sameera
see Samirah**

**Sameerah
see Samirah**

**Samia
see Samiah**

Samiah
Elevated

Samihah
Beautiful

Samimah
Sincere, true, genuine

**Samira
see Samirah**

Samirah
*Story-teller,
companion*

Samiyah
Elevated, lofty

Sana
Resplendence, brilliance

Saneeah see Sana

Saniah see Sana

Sanobar
Pine tree

Sarah
*Veil, to give joy and
happiness*

Saree see Sari

**Sareera
see Sarirah**

Sari
Most noble

Sarirah
Heart, soul

Sarwah
Wealth, prosperity

**Sarwat
see Sarwah**

**Saudah
see Sawdah**

Sawdah
Black

Sawsan
Lily of the valley (flower)

Sayyada
Star

Seema see Simah

Seemeen
see Simin

Sehar see Sihar

Shabboo
see Shabu

Shabeeba
see Shabibah

Shabiba
see Shabibah

Shabibah
Young, youthful

Shabnam
Dew

Shabu
White flower

Shad
Happy, contented

Shadha
Fragrant

Shadiya
see Shadiyah

Shadiyah
Birdsong

Shafeeah
see Shafiyah

Shafeeqah
see Shafiqah

Shafiqa
see Shafiqah

Shafiqah
Compassionate, tender,
kind-hearted

Shafiyah
Mediator

Shagoofa
see Shagufa

Shagufa
Learned

Shaheena
see Shahinah

Shahera
see Shahirah

Shahida
see Shahidah

Shahidah
Witness

Shahina
see Shahinah

Shahinah
Falcon

Shahirah
Renowned

Shahlah
Flower

Shahzadi
Princess

Shaira
see Shairah

Shairah
Poet

Shaista
see Shaistah

Shaistah
Polite, gentle

Shajeeah
see Shajiyah

Shajiyah
Courageous,
brave

Shakeelah
see Shakilah

Shakila
see Shakilah

Shakilah
Well-formed, beautiful

Shakira
see Shakirah

Shakirah
Grateful, contented

Shakoora
see Shakurah

Shakurah
Grateful

Shamamah
Scented,
fragrant

Shameela
see Shamilah

Shameelah
see Shamilah

Shameem
see Shamim

Shammemah
see Shamimah

Shamila
see Shamilah

Shamilah
Of good character

Shamim
Aroma, fragrance

Shamimah
Sweet-smelling,
fragrant

Shammee
see Shammi

Shammi
Ray of light

Shammooda
see Shamudah

Shamoodah
see Shamudah

Shamudah
Diamond

Shaqeeqa
see Shaqiqah

Shaqiqah
Sister

Sharara
Spark, flame

Shareefah
see Sharifah

Shareeka
see Sharikah

Sharfa
see Sharfah

Sharfah
Honourable

Sharifa
see Sharifah

Sharifah
Distinguished,
eminent

Sharikah
Companion, partner

Shaybah
Long life

Shayma
Noble

Shazia
see Shaziah

Shaziah
Fragrant, precious

Shereen
see Sherin

Sherin
Sweet, sugar

Shibra
see Shibrah

Shibrah
Gift, reward

Shifa
Healing

Shugofta
Blooming, flower

Shukran
*Thankful,
grateful*

Shukriyah
Thankful

Shula
Flame

Siddiqa
see Siddiqah

Siddiqah
Honest, ally, friend

Siham
Arrows

Sihar
Fascination

Simah
Sign

Simi
Silver

Simin
Silvery

Sitara
Star

Soraya
see Soriyya

Soriyya
Cluster of stars

Suad
Good fortune

Sudaqa
see Sudaqah

Sudaqah
*Friendly,
friend*

Sugheerah
see Sughrah

Sughra
see Sughrah

Saghrar
see Sughrah

Sughrah
Small, youngest

Suha
Star

Suhaila
see Suhaylah

Suhailah
see Suhaylah

Suhaima
see Suhaymah

Suhala see Suha

Suhaylah
Smooth, fluent, flowing

Suhayma
see Suhaymah

Suhaymah
Arrow

Sukainah
see Sakinah

Sulafa see Sulafah

Sulafah
Best

Sultana
see Sultanah

Sultanah
Queen

Sumaiyah
see Sumayah

Sumayah
Highness, grace

Sumayyah
see Sumayah

Sumiyya
see Sumayah

Surab
Mirage

T

Tabassum
Happiness, smile

**Tahira
see Tahirah**

Tahirah
Pure, chaste

Tahiyah
Greeting

**Tahiyya
see Tahiyah**

Tahsin
Praise

**Tahzeeb
see Tahzib**

Tahzib
*Politeness, culture,
discipline*

Taibah
Repentant

Taj
Crown

Taja see Taj

Talat
Rise

Tamim
Honest

**Tanweer
see Tanwir**

Tanwir
*Iluminate, ripen,
the morning light*

**Taqeeya
see Taqiyah**

Taqiyah
Devout, pious

**Taroob
see Tarub**

Tarub
Happy, joyful

Tasiyah
Comfort, consolation

**Taskeen
see Taskin**

Taskin
*Satisfaction,
contentment*

Tasleem
see Taslim

Taslim
Acceptance, submission

Tasneem
see Tasnim

Tasnim
Fountain in Paradise,
elevated

Taufiqa
see Tawfiqah

Tawfiqah
Prosperity, success

Taybah
Excellent

Tayibah
Pleasant, agreeable

Taysir
Making it easy

Tayyaba
see Tayibah

Tayyibah
see Tayibah

Thabita
see Thabitah

Thabitah
Firm, strong

Thameena
see Thaminah

Thameenah
see Thaminah

Thamina
see Thaminah

Thaminah
The precious one,
valuable

Thana
Praise

Tharwat
Wealth, power, influence

Thuraiya
A cluster of stars known
as 'The Seven Sisters'

Thuraiyya
see Thuraiya

Thuriyya
see Soriyya

Tohfa see Tuhfah

Tuhfah
Masterpiece

Tumadur
Brilliant, white

Ulfah
*Love, friendship,
harmony*

Ulfat see Ulfah

Ulima
The learned one

Ulimah see Ulima

Umaymah
Ahead, in front

Umm
Mother

Urwah
Support

Uzma
Greatest, best

Waddiya
see **Waddiyah**

Waddiyah
*Friendly, amicable,
gentle*

Wadeeda
see **Waddiyah**

Wadidah
see **Waddiyah**

Wafa
Faithfulness, loyalty

Wafeeqa
see **Wafiqah**

Wafeeya
see **Wafiyah**

Wafiqah
Successful

Wafiya
see **Wafiyah**

Wafiyah
Loyal, faithful

Wafiyyah
see **Wafiyah**

Waheeda
see **Wahidah**

Waheedah
see **Wahidah**

Wahibah
Provider, giver

Wahidah
Unique, exclusive

Wajida
see **Wajidah**

Wajidah
*Achiever, one who
endeavours*

Wajiha
see **Wajihah**

Wajihah
Eminent, distinguished

Waleeda
see **Walidah**

Walidah
Newborn, baby

Waliyah
Ruler

Waliyya
see Waliyah

Wardad
see Wardah

Wardah
Red rose, brave

Warithah
Heir

Waseefa
see Wasifah

Waseemah
see Wasimah

Wasifah
Servant

Wasima
see Wasimah

Wasimah
Pretty, graceful

Widad
Love, friendship

Wijdan
Sentiment, emotion

Wisal
Love, friendship

Yamama
see Yamamah

Yamamah
Dove

Yaqoot
see Yaqut

Yaqut
Sapphire

Yasamin
see Yasmin

Yasemin
see Yasmin

Yasmeen
see Yasmin

Yasmin
Fragrant flower
(jasmine)

Yasmina
see Yasmin

Yasmine
see Yasmin

Yasoob see Yasub

Yasub
Queen bee

Yumn see Yumnah

Yumnah
Fortunate, lucky

Yusra
Prosperous

Z

Zada
The lucky one

Zadah see Zada

Zafaran
Saffron (herb)

Zafirah
*Victorious,
successful*

**Zaheera
see Zahirah**

Zahidah
*Self-denying, to devote
oneself to Allah*

Zahirah
Shining, in full bloom

Zahra
Courage, beautiful

**Zahrah
see Zahra**

Zaib
Beauty

Zaiba
Beautiful

Zaibun
The most beautiful

Zaida see Zaidah

Zaidah
Growing, increasing, prosperous

Zaimah
Leader

**Zainab
see Zaynab**

Zainab
A beautiful and fragrant tree

**Zaitoon
see Zaitun**

**Zaitoonah
see Zaitunah**

Zaitun
Olive tree

Zaitunah
Olive

Zakirah
Devout, pious

Zakiyah
Honest, perceptive

**Zakiyyah
see Zakiyah**

**Zakkiya
see Zakiyah**

**Zaleekhah
see Zulaikhah**

Zara
Splendour, brightness, dawn

Zarina
Golden

Zarqa
Blue

Zayb see Zaib

**Zayba
see Zaiba**

Zaynah
Type of tree, beautiful

Zaynah
Beautiful

**Zaytoon
see Zaytunah**

Zayttona
see Zaytunah

Zaytun
see Zaytunah

Zaytunah
Olive

Zeenat see Zinah

Zinah
Beauty, adornment

Zohra see Zuhrah

Zubaida
see Zubaydah

Zubaidah
see Zubaydah

Zubaydah
The cream of the crop,
radiant

Zuharah
see Zuhrah

Zuhra see Zuhrah

Zuhrah
Beauty, splendour

Zulaikha
see Zulaikhah

Zulaikhah
Beautiful, fair

Zuleika
see Zulaikhah

Zuleikah
see Zulaikhah

NOTES

Other titles published by Hansib Publications